Vim and Vig

By Carmel Reilly

T0360253

Vig is an ant.

Vim is an ant, too.

Vig and Vim run and run.

Vig lugs a big bit
of jam bun.

Vim lugs a bit of bun, too.

Vig and Vim run up
the wet log.

Vim hops off the log.

Vig hops, but ...

Vig hits a big web!

The jam bun hits the web!

Vim runs up the wet log.

She jets in to the web.

Vim and Vig hit the mud.

Vim got a rod
and hit the web.

The jam bun hit the mud.

CHECKING FOR MEANING

1. What sort of bun does Vig lug? *(Literal)*

2. What does Vim use to get the bun out of the web? *(Literal)*

3. How would you describe the character of Vim? *(Inferential)*

EXTENDING VOCABULARY

wet	Look at the word *wet*. What is the middle sound in this word? Find another word in the book that has the same sound in the middle.
lugs	The word *lugs* means to carry or drag. What sorts of things might you *lug* around?
to	Find another word in the book that sounds the same as *to* but is spelled differently. What do each of the words mean?

MOVING BEYOND THE TEXT

1. Where do ants usually live?

2. How many legs do insects have? What else do you know about them?

3. What other insects might you find in a garden?

4. What might have happened if Vim didn't rescue Vig from the web? How do you know this?

SPEED SOUNDS

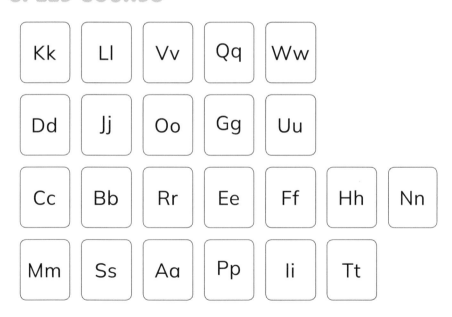

Kk Ll Vv Qq Ww

Dd Jj Oo Gg Uu

Cc Bb Rr Ee Ff Hh Nn

Mm Ss Aa Pp Ii Tt

PRACTICE WORDS

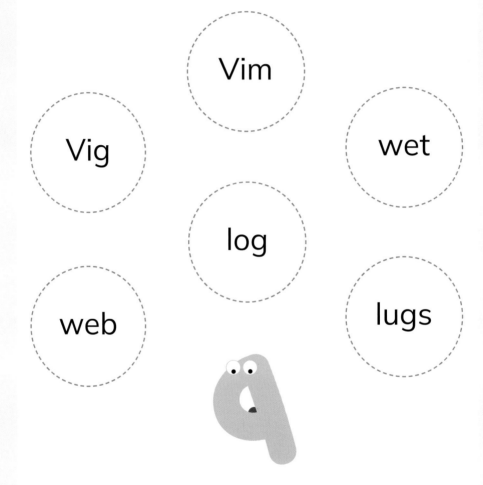

Vim

Vig

wet

log

web

lugs